apple

Apfel

pear

Birne

orange

Orange

lemon

Zitrone

grapes

Weintrauben

strawberry

Erdbeere

watermelon

Wassermelone

coconut

Kokosnuss

banana

Banane

raspberry

Himbeere

kiwi

Kiwi

cherry

Kirsche

blueberry

Heidelbeere

plum

Pflaume

peach

Pfirsich

fig

Feige

pineapple

Ananas

mango

Mango

persimmon

Kaki

cauliflower

Blumenkohl

zucchini

Zucchini

eggplant

Aubergine

carrot

Karotte

potato

Kartoffel

cabbage

Kohl

tomato

Tomate

spinach

Spinat

broccoli

Brokkoli

peas

Erbsen

pumpkin

Kürbis

butternut squash

Butternusskürbis

avocado

Avocado

artichoke

Artischocke

mushroom

Pilz

radish

Radieschen

garlic

Knoblauch

onion

Zwiebel

beet

Rote Beete

leek

Lauch

bell pepper

Paprika

chili pepper

Chilischoten

asparagus

Spargel